The Ramblings of a Little Lost Soul

The Ramblings of a Little Lost Soul

Jean Tymms

Matador
9 Priory Business Park,
Wistow Road, Kibworth Beauchamp,
Leicestershire. LE8 0RX
Tel: 0116 279 2299
Email: books@troubador.co.uk
Web: www.troubador.co.uk/matador
Twitter: @matadorbooks

ISBN 978 1785891 090

British Library Cataloguing in Publication Data.
A catalogue record for this book is available from the British Library.

Printed and bound by CPI Group (UK) Ltd, Croydon, CR0 4YY
Typeset in 11pt Adobe Garamond Pro by Troubador Publishing Ltd, Leicester, UK

Matador is an imprint of Troubador Publishing Ltd

In memory of my very dear husband, Geoff

7th March 1935 - 16th January 2014

I missed him then,
I miss him still
Somehow I know I always will
– more and more each day

Foreword

My brother Geoff and his wife Jean were known by some of the villagers of Dunster as Romeo and Juliet as they went about their business with his arm around her or hand in hand. I cannot imagine what 'Juliet' must have felt when, metaphorically speaking, her balcony came crashing down and Romeo was no longer on this earth.

This book is written by Jean to relieve her own pain but also in the hope that sharing her grief might help others in a similar position and is dedicated to all those suffering (both cared for and caring) from any form of cancer.

Jean has stated that a large percentage of any profits arising from the book will go to charities close to her heart and in particular Myeloma UK as Geoff died of myeloma – a cancer of the bone marrow, about which there is still a lot to be learnt.

ROY TYMMS

Introduction

When I saw my husband smiling at me, trying not to show how much pain he was in it felt like my heart was in a vice, which was tightening a bit more every day. Myeloma, this agonising form of cancer – about which so much is still not known – needed a bit more research. I could not bear to think of anyone else going through so much pain and stress, hence the fundraising. It was not meant to be this way either. We were firmly convinced we would go together. Somewhere along the way we must have slipped "off course" because it did not happen, however much we wanted it to.

Then followed bereavement, and the, "You will get over it in time", "It gets easier after a while". Not so. Following this you have the people who go the long way round, rather than to talk to you. Not because they are horrid people, but just that they do not know what to say and in their heart of hearts, I would guess, do not want to cause you any more hurt. I began to talk to a lot of others who had been in my circumstances, for some, their loss was many years ago and they confirmed what I have just said, plus many other little things that have hurt them. Not least the assumption that we are all the same and therefore affected the same way. Again, not so. I guess it all stems from the scientific "logical thought"! But we are all very different in the way we react to certain issues, and this one in particular. When we leave our "case" behind, our soul, spirit, whatever you wish to call it, goes on. It is this that makes us so individual and each one needs a different approach to help them.

I was like a zombie on the outside; I was always crying, lost all my confidence, afraid of everything, whilst inside I felt such anger and heartbreak that he should be taken from me. Then a little voice said, 'Write it all down exactly as you think and feel it.' So I came to scribbling things down with the thought that I was telling it all to a stranger, and this gave me an outlet. I am so glad that I did, as it has helped me beyond belief. The peak of my story being the trip to Austria. You will never know how big a challenge I had set myself, but it worked. I have surprised myself. I found my way round okay, tried out my German on some poor unsuspecting Austrians, went up the mountain on the train, and attacked getting to the top with a determination I forgot I had. I found I could laugh again. Not in the gut way, as with Geoff, but with a sort of happiness. Thus I have started to walk on a "me" path, with things still to learn and do. I must admit I have two parallel paths: mine on earth, and the one with Geoff in spirit because when you have spent close on sixty years together and loving each other so much, they are both likely to merge together, especially with my tour as my old memories soon became interlocked with the new ones I was making. The story I have written closes here, close on to sixteen months after he died. But a new story is beginning. The one I shall write just for me.

For those who are recently bereaved, or are facing it in the near future I send my love and wishes that my little book may help and that you get the love, support and caring that you need.

To others reading this I would ask that you talk to the

bereaved person in the same old way. We love the opportunity of talking about our dear ones, and yes, there may be a tear of two at the beginning, but inadvertently you are helping them onto the path of healing and self-awareness. I can only speak for myself, of course, but it helped me. I know it is difficult sometimes, even my children on occasions do not know what to say to help me, but just speaking to me naturally does. Also having good, understanding friends help, and I was fortunate enough to have some.

Love and blessings to all who are walking this path.

JEAN

The days drag by
As with each memory I cry
But crying does not ease the pain.
That will only go when we are together.
The day you hold out your hand to me
I will not want to weep again.

Jean Tymms

How I Remember You

Your smiling face looking down to mine as you hold me tight,
Walking together beneath the stars,
Everything feeling right.
Wedding bells, honeymoon,
Vows taken and meant so true.
These are the memories, my Geoff, I have of you.

Walking in the hills holding hands,
or along the Cornish cliff paths.
Laughing and joking with the kids,
or at the pub with the "boys".
Standing stones, dowsing rods,
or in shorts running off into the wilds.
These are the memories, my Geoff, I have of you.

"Jack and Jill" watching our children growing up,
then going on their way,
Life a ray of lovely colours and beautiful music as we share every day,
Once so young, then together, growing old,
Sharing our lives, which have been so full of joy.
These are my memories,
My darling Geoff, I have of you.

How wonderful life was when you were on this earth with me.

1. The Ramblings of a Little Lost Soul

The creamery supervisor's daughter and the bank manager's son saw each other across a room and knew they wanted to spend their lives together. Sounds corny! Nevertheless it is very true. This is the story of bereavement. How two people made a wonderful life together until, in a way, they both died.

In the 50s, I was working in the office of a woodworking machinery company in central London. We needed an assistant manager and one day, in response to an ad in the paper, this lovely smiling chap came for an interview and was given the post. As he was being shown around we looked up into each other's eyes and knew we wanted to be together for always. Geoff told me later I smiled up at him and stole his heart away. Couldn't have described it better, as that was exactly what I had felt. We soon, in a matter of months, got engaged. He wasn't the get-down-on-one-knee-type, it was just 'When we get married…'

I remember saying, 'Haven't you forgotten something such as asking me the question?' He chuckled and said, 'You will, won't you?'

That was much the way it was throughout our married life. We took a lot of knocks in our long life together: two of our children having serious illnesses and the concern that our other two should not feel left out because of the attention needed by our poorly two; shortage of cash at times; and all those sort of things that other married couples get. But we had a bonus. Geoff's mum was the most wonderful friend to both of us and was always there when needed.

Sadly working life was not fulfilling for him. He did it well but it was a terrible strain on him and was really only done to provide for his family. His outlet was long-distance running. I soon got used to seeing the back end of him running off to the hills and the pile of sweaty washing when he got back. Those were important times for him and enabled him to find the answers to any problem he had. Needless to say I did not run up in the hills. I was too busy running around after the kiddies and looking after their needs. Life was very happy. We had the same thoughts and frequently said the same thing at the same time. We shared the same likes and dislikes in the main. It was not always a garden of roses though. If he got a bee in his bonnet he could be as stubborn as a mule – but he would suddenly give one of his smiles, put his arm around my shoulders and all was forgotten. For the time being anyway. So life went on in its humdrum way. Thanks to Geoff's mum and dad living by the sea, we had three or four lovely breaks each year, which have brought about a massive store of memories. Mainly good but some were bittersweet, one being the death of his mother in 1976. Apart from the loss of my nan this was the first time I had come face to face with bereavement and the pain it can bring. Mum was my pal and I could talk to her about anything. Needless to say it hit Geoff hard too. It left quite a gap in our lives and, for my part she is still deeply missed.

As time went on our little fledglings flew the nest. Our eldest married a girl he had met at school and they have just celebrated thirty-five years of marriage. They have two lovely children; a boy and a girl. Both of whom we love dearly – nearly as much as we love our own brood. Over the years we have had our tiffs and differences, as families do, but in essence we are one big family full of love and caring; our four lovely children, all of whom are so very different, love each other dearly and we are so very proud of them, their partners and children. We have always loved them to bits.

Geoff and I both had quite demanding jobs, and over a long period they became too demanding. Our friend and family doctor told us we must change our way of life. The "or else" was so strong we found ourselves on the move and, as if by divine intervention, found ourselves a house in Dunster. Admittedly, a house that needed a lot of tender loving care – a bit crazy considering we were both unwell. But it is strange how things work out. The villagers and neighbours were so kind and helpful to us. When we ran out of cash, means of earning were presented to us. The house grew more warm and beautiful with each day. However, the most important thing was that we felt we had at last come home. Everything felt so familiar, so right. Eventually we set up as a little B&B house and Geoff topped up funds with some consultancy work. Everything was wonderful and we were so happy. We loved Somerset's moors and sea – in fact, just everything. We were given to taking lovely long walks, which we later shared with our guests. It was a lovely way of meeting the world.

The first crack in our dream world was when Geoff became ill. They found it difficult to find out what his problem was. Eventually a large tumour was found in his left kidney and they had to operate. During this procedure he lost his spleen also, hence his immune system was very weak and he needed ten yearly vaccinations. All might have been well if he had not agreed to take over the offices in Bristol and go back to doing the work he did before. He said "only for two years" but it went into six and, although everything had been fine up until then, what with the stress of the job and the very long hours of driving to and fro, it was obvious his health was suffering and so this operation came about. It took six months to really get him back on his feet again. For fifteen more years all was great. Geoff had found himself to be a pretty good dowser – and in the true Geoff style wanted to dowse every standing stone circle, very old houses, earth energies, ley lines and the effect they have on people and animals. He wrote reams of notes, drawings and so forth with the intention of writing a book on the subject. I became involved in healing, and as was the way with Geoff and I, we were soon deeply involved with each other's work and becoming part of it. This period was such an adventure for us, and the healing and dowsing became an integral part of our lives – we loved it.

The first very noticeable sign that all was not well with Geoff was in around 2010. We were taken by our son and grandson to Chartres in France for our fiftieth wedding anniversary. When in Chartres Cathedral, we wanted to walk the labyrinth but he suddenly found his legs would not hold him up, felt odd too. We sat him down for a while and as soon as he felt brighter I walked it with him. He managed it but it was clear he needed to lean on me quite a lot. By the next day he was okay again and was so for quite a while – until it happened again. Gradually it got that his thinking was confused and he was more fearful of doing some things that had never bothered him before. He couldn't put his paperwork in order or get on with his book. It was all so distressing. This was not all of the time, it was in patches; the rest of the time he was okay, which made it even more distressing to see it happening. This beautiful, loving, clever man was becoming very ill and more dependent and we really did not know why.

Then came the day when our world stopped still. Myeloma was diagnosed. Apparently not an easy ailment to spot but it did not take us long to realise that this was very serious for someone with a weakened immune system. This happened in January 2013. For a long period he was having bouts of being unable to remember things, getting confused, distressed and frustrated. He had a number of falls as his legs lost all strength on occasions. He crashed into the cooker and injured his head during one of these falls and I thought he was going to pass away then but, as it is with myeloma they gave him some medication and within an hour he was really quite perky, and you could almost believe it had never happened. A few days later and he was home from hospital. For a little while we were able to go for walks again but, all too soon, the weakness in his legs started to show. Also he had problems with some of the medication, which added to his weakness. Slowly but surely his condition deteriorated.

On one of his bright days, my eldest son and his wife took us to Arlington House. We had a super time. Geoff was really enjoying himself and walking well. At about one o'clock it was suggested we set off to get some lunch. Just a few minutes into our journey to the cafe Geoff told me he felt odd. I knew the signs and immediately told my son to turn the car round and head for home – which was on the other side of the Exmoor moors, in less than half an hour my darling was like a rag doll – no control over his limbs. Even his head wobbled and the whites of his eyes just seemed to be disappearing. We rang the paramedics straightaway but there was a delay getting to us. We were told to get him out of the vehicle ready for them, but it was a nightmare trying. He could not help us and had got himself wedged between the seats but, with the aid of two kindly passers-by, we did finally get him out and put him in a sitting position. The paramedics arrived and he was rushed to hospital. We all felt this time we had lost him, even the medics thought so, but once again, he was given treatment and was quite bright again. We had him home again within three days. However, this time he began to slide downhill. The little walks to the tea room became harder and harder. He began to lose control over bladder and bowels. Getting upstairs or even into the bathroom became a major operation. But worse of all was his distress. He suffered some experiences in hospital that he had found humiliating. He was frustrated and finding it hard to understand what was happening to him. Extra little bumps appeared on his back and ribs. Even his eyes changed shape. It was all heartbreaking. Eventually he was taken into our local hospital where he found such love and compassion as they tended to him. On 8th January, my birthday, my daughter and I were told he had not much time left. My world just fell apart. I stayed with him day and night and held his hand. He fought like mad. He didn't want to leave us but it was out of the hands of us all. On 16th January 2014 he quietly passed away and took a large part of me with him.

During this time we had the love of our four children surrounding and supporting us, along with cards and calls from grandchildren and friends. Our daughter and her husband lived nearby and were wonderful, giving lifts to and from hospitals and any number of other things, and our lads, who all live quite a way from home, visited and kept in touch and did all they could. I know they all felt crushed by his demise – heartbroken. With all the sadness I still feel grateful to have been able to love and care for him all the way to the end and recall that even then he left treasured memories. On my birthday I had dressed up for him and put on perfume. He seemed in a sleep state most of the time so when I said, 'Bet you can't smell this.' I was amazed to get, 'I can,' and he gave a meow sound Roy Orbison would have been proud of. It was really cheeky and I will hold that moment close to me always. Lastly, as my daughter was leaving she heard him say, 'Night, night.' His last words ever on this earth that we would hear. He had such a soft gentle voice most of the time. I was holding his hand as he passed on.

After that, everything was chaos in my mind and body. I had never envisaged a life without him. We even thought we would go together. Such energy was being pulled through my hands by him I truly believe he tried to take me with him but it was not meant to be. I know many will laugh or shun this statement but it was as I have written. Many others will understand it. For quite a few days there was no time to think, so many things had to be done; funeral, cremation, stone and interment of ashes, meals for family and friends and places to stay. Letting everyone know of his death. It seemed to go on and on.

We had a very simple service and a wicker coffin, which, somehow, looked less harsh than the traditional ones do. It told a short story of our lives ending with "Lark Ascending" and I could feel his freedom from earthly pain as the music reached its heights. Apparently all present understood what we were trying to say, which was rather special. We delayed the interment of Geoff's ashes until his birthday. We thought we would give him a final party. We went to the Garden of Rest and our priest friend said the prayers and then my family – children and grandchildren – each made their own personal farewell to him. We each put a small present in with him as we said our farewell. All very emotional and very touching. Too personal to put into words here. Suddenly my youngest son said how he and his wife had been thinking of Geoff and his brother Roy's love of *The Goons*. They used to take off two of the characters so well you could hardly tell the difference between them and the professionals. He went on to say, 'So Gina is going to make some comments and then show some cards and you must all do exactly what the cards and Gina say you should do.' She started by telling one or two little Goon jokes, and then came the first card. When I saw what was written on it I thought, *they can't be thinking of doing what I think they are going to do!* The second card made it quite clear that was exactly what they were going to do. They had all of us singing the 'Ying Tong' song and drinking a toast with Guinness in little glasses. Such a silly thing but strangely right. For just a moment we forgot about the sadness and remembered the joy his life gave to many and the happiness and love we have had and still feel from him.

After the interment party I went home with my youngest son and his wife for a week. They looked after me and took me around and about but I found everything very bewildering for within myself I seemed to have lost all my strength and confidence. I felt scared I was going to get lost when we went out. Such crazy stuff – but then this was the first time I had gone away without Geoff by my side or at least with the knowledge that he would not be waiting for me or coming home to me. I was really a very lost soul. When I got home, feeling a little better – sort of – I was faced with a will, which I have dealt with before, Inland Revenue, pensions, services, water rates, notifying people so they would stop sending their details, requests and God knows what else, all of which I hadn't dealt with for many years. In this computerised world it was a nightmare, on top of the nightmare I was already living. Distress levels got pretty high. It seemed impossible to speak to anyone I wanted to. It was all numbered options, none of which related to what I wanted. I was constantly in tears and really didn't want to be here at all. I just wanted to be with my Geoff, which was very hard for my family. My weight went down quite a lot and I didn't always feel like eating. Sometimes I just forgot to. I walked for miles. I couldn't bear to be indoors. Bless him, my second son had bought me a surprise gift, which was presented to me whilst we had a coffee before the stone was put into place. He said I could find the world on it and in time, when I got used to it, I could talk to them all and see them, which might make things a little easier. It was a Samsung Tablet, and has really helped me so much. I've learned how to send emails, find music, TV and games on it so far. Telephone yet to come. I guess I have used it to block out my thoughts, almost switch off completely.

I constantly "talk" to Geoff. I've been through every emotion in the book; could I have done more for him? Will he be with me still? Will he be there when I pass on? Then I've cried enough to fill an ocean followed by pure anger – Why didn't you take me with you? Quite natural things for me to do, I'm told, but it felt strangely personal and like it was only happening to me. I wasn't feeling lonely – I was feeling alone. We were soul mates and had known each other for sixty years, married for the greater part. We loved each other dearly and he has left a great hole in my being that can never be filled – never!

It is nearly eight months since he passed away. I am trying to make sense of everything. I'm on a seeking path now, trying to find my way. I am told I have things to do. I'm looking for them. I meet lovely people for coffee, or give healing to. I go out with my family and I do enjoy doing these things but somehow everything I do just emphasises the greatness of my loss. I miss him totally and often find myself crying, sometimes without obvious reason, sometimes through a piece of music or just seeing a couple walking along holding hands.

At Geoff's funeral I decided that only family should send flowers. It came to me that perhaps we could raise money for a charity that would be caring for people like Geoff and finding new and more gentle ways of curing myeloma. My son Ken found just one, Myeloma UK, whom I contacted. They were the most gentle and caring of people. I spoke to a gentlemen for quite a long while and ended with a feeling of purpose. Some good could come out of it all. They have helped me all the way and thanks to the response from family, friends, church, local shops and numerous other wonderful caring people we raised a good sum of money for them. This was my little bit of light in the darkness. We haven't stopped this funding as a good friend of ours is doing a sponsored jump so help will continue. For my part, I am trying to get to know myself and trying to get the courage to go on alone, which is what we have to do. Our youngsters have their own lives to lead and can only do so much. I still cry a lot, feel alone and sometimes feel pretty desperate but somewhere out there there are things for me to do with my life. I know this grief I feel will never go but get manageable. I liken myself to the phoenix in *Harry Potter*; when Geoff died, 80% of me died also; everything I knew, did, or went to died with him but a little patch of ashes remain, and like the phoenix, I must rise out of the ashes and learn to live again and go forth into a rather lonely and scary world to prove I am capable of making a new life for myself until he holds his hand out to me and we can be together again.

My beautiful children

2. The Slow Rising of the Phoenix

It is now some six months since my darling went into his last earthly sleep, leaving me alone and lost.

I am not sure where they get the idea that things will get easier, at least, more tolerable. Over the past six months, I was certainly not finding that at all. It was getting more painful as I began to accept that things would never be the same. He would not be there when I came home from the shops, his smiling face looking up at me. Would not be in the chair beside me, holding my hand as we watched TV together, and I would not feel his arms enfold me, giving me comfort and love when I was distressed or just very tired. It really would never be the same. It was a nightmare that would not go away. I never realised just how unhappy a person can be, until now. Life is just not worth living without my dear one by my side. I must admit that I do have happy periods, happy times, but at the end of them I feel the loss of Geoff even deeper, of really being alone. Dinner to cook? What is the point without Geoff there to share it? I cannot raise any interest in cooking, home, or anything else just for myself. It was the love and sharing life with each other that made life joyful, not looking after myself.

I have been learning things about myself, as I guess I was meant to! Fundraising was a thing I never thought I could do, being a bit shy, and yet the one thing that has kept me sane has been two slots of fundraising for research into myeloma for Myeloma UK, this being the illness that took my husband from me. I raised a respectable amount with aid from my family and friends, and then teamed up with a friend of mine to organise a sponsored event. Initially it was going to be quite modest but my dear pal pulled out all the stops, and, with the aid of her charity-working team, organised a fantastic coast steering event, which has kept growing and growing. I think Myeloma UK will get a goodly sum towards their research work in due course.

I also find that I can express myself fairly well through the pen, writing what is in my heart. Perhaps I still have something to offer in memory of my lovely Geoff.

All the above has helped, but not enough to fill the huge void his passing has left me with.

The turning point came when Ken rang and said he was taking me away for one week's holiday. 'Where would you like to go?' he asked. I told him I would like to go to Cornwall. Ken was hesitant as he knew Geoff and I went there often, but this was my treat from him and my brother-in-law so he went along with it. He rented a bungalow in Mullion near the Lizard Point – such a happy place for Geoff and I.

On a lovely September evening we arrived at our home for the week: a lovely bungalow, in a quiet setting, with a view of the sea. It was heavenly. My dear son generously let me have the big double room as it had the sea view, and he was aware of my affinity with the sea. We settled in and went for a meal at the local inn, followed by watching a film together at the bungalow – such a comfortable start to our break. I must admit, I cried myself to sleep that night. I so longed to cuddle up to my Geoff and found his absence virtually unbearable.

I awoke in the morning and was greeted with a lovely cup of tea and a divine morning with sun shining over the blue-green sea full of sparkling diamonds. I felt happy. At this point in time, this was the right place for me to be.

After we had breakfast, Ken had to finish off some office work so I had a couple of hours to myself. I went for a stroll around the village going onto the coastal walk, where I breathed in the pure air and took in all the beauty around me. How the memories started to flood in. Such happy memories in the main. I was reminded of all the joyful and wonderful things we had shared in our lives.

Our first home was a bungalow on a high hill in Chesham, Buckinghamshire. We had very little in the way of possessions. A second-hand suite for the princely sum of ten pounds. A fridge provided by an elderly aunt – a real antique – and an ancient washer with rollers, and so on, but we were pleased with everything and were so chuffed as we saved up, and eventually replaced them. We and our four children were happy there. Our own home at last.

It got pretty hard sometimes. One year the snow was so bad we were unable to get to the shop. Imagine our delight when the grocery man turned up at 10pm with all our goods on a sleigh. It felt like Father Christmas had come early. It had its funny side too. Sometimes when it got really cold our doors and windows froze solid and we could not open them, save one, and from this one Geoff, in all his office gear, would climb out and set off to work, complete with his briefcase.

Here we had tests and trials to. One summer our eldest son, just seven years of age, began to find it difficult to walk because of pains in his groin. Thank God I have always been a little intuitive, as I felt sure this was more than just a little boy not wanting to go to school. The doctor confirmed this and put us in touch with a specialist. He and the doctor came to our home a couple of days later. What he told us was alarming, but once he had judged that we were able to cope he told us of what he actually hoped for. Our lad was to be in hospital for three weeks and then to wear callipers and irons for the duration of the illness. Apparently this condition went through a cycle, and as we had spotted it early it took three years to heal. He was such a brave little chap and tried everything. I was more than a little shaken to see him riding down the road on a bike, his good leg pedalling at a great rate of knots and his affected leg sticking out like a knight's lance. The local children called him the "fastest hop in the west". Could he move!

One very touching things comes to mind. When my Nigel was in hospital he was told that when he put his callipers and irons on, and, once he was able to walk the length of the ward, he could go home. My very determined lad, on the very first try, did just that, but by the time he was driven home he could barely make it down the path to the house. It brought tears to everyone's eyes. Indoors our little Susie, of about ten months, was playing in her playpen. When her brother came through the door she smiled and held her arms up to him. We took off his callipers and irons, gently sat him in the playpen for a while with her and they just cuddled up to each other. It really was one of those very special moments in life.

A strange thing came out of all this. After the specialist had left, I went into a deep sleep. Nobody could wake me up and, as I was usually a very light sleeper, this worried everyone to bits. When I awoke, some two hours later, I seemed to know exactly what to do and how to care for Nigel with the certainty of a fully trained nurse. This was to happen again a year later when my youngest son, Mark was born, with another rare illness. He was very ill. His body was not functioning properly and after a biopsy it was found that a large part of his intestine was without nerves. He had to have a colostomy, which he had until just before he was two years old. He was a pretty baby with auburn hair but he never cried or wanted to eat. I had such a shock when I saw him in hospital after his first operation. He had lost most of his beautiful hair, his face was all eyes and he looked as if he had been cut in half, the wound was so big, but he was crying for attention, and food. Our baby was fighting back. As if that was not enough during that period, our poor little Sue had a perforated ear drum, which has left her with a monotone sound in one ear, and our Ken, after being stung by a wasp, putting him almost into a coma, was found to be seriously allergic. Luckily we got him to a doctor in time. A truly testing time when we really found out what we were made of!

Over the years I began to wonder if these events were perhaps preparing me for the biggest change in my life I could have foreseen. But what it was I did not know at the time.

I am looking down at Mullion Harbour now. The rocks and foaming waves are beautiful. I love the quick changes of the mood of the sea here. One minute serene and calm, quite quickly turning into huge, rolling, angry waves and high winds. The wildness of it all is magical. It holds me in awe and respect, but also brings peace to my soul. At the moment, my memories are quiet for a while. It feels as if it was a long time since the last visit here but it was just a short eighteen months ago that we were here together. He was getting a little weaker then.

Geoff looking at Mullion Cove from our holiday bungalow.
Never without his pipe

Time to go back to the bungalow and my Kennie, and see where we go for the rest of the day.

We decided to go to Cadgwith Cove, a dear little fishing village with a very pleasant inn. We had to park our car up at the top and walk down a really unusual path where there are a few cottages and a peaceful fishermen's chapel. I love it there and have often popped in for a quiet moment of prayer and meditation. On this occasion we made a visit to the inn and had an enjoyable drink whilst looking at the sea and the fishing boats. Here you can buy fish directly from the sea. Smashing!

I am looking forward to tomorrow. We are going on the walk that I so desperately want to do again, just once more whilst I am still able. Ever since Geoff died I have wanted, indeed needed, to get back to Cornwall, and in particular the Lizard Point where our walk always started. It is one we did many, many times and really loved it. We would set off from Lizard village to Church Cove, then along the coastal path to the Point and thereon complete the circuit back to the village. We never failed to feel anything but pure joy on this walk. The sea, the rocks, the profusion of wild multi-coloured flowers, the nooks and crannies, changing all the time, and the large standing stones ,which drew Geoff – and his rods – to them like a magnet. When we arrived at the Point we would stop at the delightful little cafe on the edge where I always had a Horlicks with my meal, whatever the weather, and Geoff enjoyed his usual coffee. We would peacefully look out to sea at the fascinating formation of the rocks with the birds diving from them or flying over to see what we had to spare. Occasionally we had the good fortune to see a playful seal, always a joy to watch. Then there were the ships and boats of varying shapes and sizes, wondering where they came from and what their destination was. What a moving magical picture.

Now, here we are, Ken and I walking along together in the footsteps of the past. It is as lovely as ever and I feel Geoff with us all the time, as if trying to remind me of all those wonderful things we learnt and experienced together, and the joy they gave us, such as my healing gift and Geoff's discovery of dowsing.

Many times over the years I have been told I had clairvoyant and healing abilities. I cannot say I took it too seriously as I felt I was not worthy of such gifts – soon this was all about to change.

Geoff came home from work one day and told me he was passing lots of blood in his water. He did not know what to do. He had just driven for two hours in this condition and was alarmed, tired and in shock. We contacted our doctor and we were soon on our way to the hospital. By this time the blood had coagulated and he was unable to pass anything at all, causing him a lot of pain. They flushed him through, attached him to a bag and made him as comfortable as possible. He was kept in hospital over the Christmas period and being given a lot of tests. They were finding it difficult to find the problem. They eventually decided it was his prostate gland and needed an operation. He had just seen the anaesthetist ready to go into the theatre when I got a really powerful voice saying, 'This is not right, it is his kidney.' It was very persistent so I approached the sister and told her I felt it may not be his prostate and thought it could be his kidney. I expected to be put in my place but the sister put her arm around my shoulders and asked why I thought this. I just said I keep getting this feeling and I do recall he used to get aches in that area of his body sometimes. Bless her. After some thought she had the operation cancelled and Geoff was given some more tests, the outcome of which was to find a large tumour in his left kidney.

His operation seemed to take a long time and I was getting concerned. Apparently so was the sister who was on the phone to the theatre about it. He was just coming out into the recovery room and I was allowed to be with him.

He was thrashing about, looking in a bad way and somehow I knew they had done more than was expected. I remember saying to him, 'Calm down, darling, they have obviously had to do a little more than they had thought and your body is in shock. I am not allowed to stay with you for long.' However, a voice from behind me told me to stay where I was as I was doing very well. As he went into the main ward the theatre nurse told me they had also removed his spleen! I was able to stay with him all through the night and all the next day. He had cardiac arrest three times and I began to feel I was going to lose him. He hung on to my hand all the time, even though he was unconscious. The nurses asked me to give the reading on his blood pressure monitor. I kept thinking if we can just get him through to six am, he will be ok. Why do I feel this so strongly?

During this time I began to get pains in both of my arms. I thought I was heading for a heart attack. Then a strange thing happened. At spot on six am, Geoff came round. He opened his eyes, looked at me, and said, 'Jeannie, please put your hands on my back as I am in such pain.' I really was not quite sure what to do so I just put my hands side by side onto his back. To my amazement the pains I was feeling in my hands and arms became a sort of energy, which flowed to my fingers and into Geoff's back. It was like electricity and my arms immediately felt fine. I was wondering whatever was going on and what made Geoff ask me to put my hands on him, but as I saw that Geoff had fallen asleep and was looking calm and peaceful. I just stopped thinking about it for a while. I was with Geoff most of the time over the next three days and he was doing well.

In the meantime, I had not had much sleep and did not

feel like eating. My mind was in a whirl. 8th January was my birthday and my daughter took me out for a meal. We went but it did not happen as I felt tired, confused, unwell and just wanted to get home. My poor little daughter, after all her efforts. Back home I was to get a few more surprises. My lovely neighbour Rose asked me what had happened at the hospital and asked after Geoff. When I told her all about it she had a little chuckle and said, 'My dear, your healing power has come through.' Now totally confused I asked her what she meant. She went on to tell me that a healing lady, who worked with Harry Edwards used to live in the house opposite. One day this lady came to tell her she was moving to Guildford to work more closely with Harry at the sanctuary. She had gone on to tell Rose that she was not to worry as a lady would be moving in next door who would be her next healer. Apparently when Rose saw me moving in she knew I was the one but was equally aware that I was not aware of it. I took myself off to bed now totally bewildered. *What the dickens is happening to me?*

I climbed into bed and there at the end of the bed I saw a beautiful figure of a being just looking at me. I did not know whether it was male or female only that it was very special, angelic, Christ-like even and so full of colours and transparent, for want of a better word to use. I closed my eyes and thought I must be heading for a breakdown. When I open my eyes it will be gone but when I opened them it was still there gently looking at me, and the light was even brighter. It emanated such love, such peace and caring I curled up and had a wonderful and restful sleep, and awoke feeling stronger, almost ready for anything. Almost!

Geoff told me later that when I put my hands on his back it felt like a warm tingly sort of current going up and down his back taking the pain away, never to return. He also told me that his assistant's wife was a clairvoyant and kept telling him that Geoff's wife was a fully-fledged healer and should be working now. She was pretty persistent on the subject when I later met her. It would seem I was the only one who did not know?

Having been kick-started, my healing ability grew stronger and Rose saw to it that I used it and developed it further. Whenever she was unwell she would pop in to me, and the word just seemed to get around. My poor old Geoff, a bit hard on him being the starting point to all this, but he was so happy about the outcome and had regular healing sessions himself. I guess I should have questioned why I used to get very hot hands, and kept putting them under the cold tap to cool them down!

I took Geoff for a few days' convalescence in the Austrian Tyrol in May. His progress was phenomenal. The mountain air did wonders for him. I just could not keep up with him. It was wonderful.

It was only a couple of years later that we got involved in dowsing and it was brought to us by two American guests at our bed and breakfast establishment. An amazing thing happened. One sunny afternoon two ladies came to stay with us, a really charming couple. One of them was always deeply engrossed in a book she had with her. Being book lovers ourselves we were rather keen to know what it was about. We were not to be disappointed as the young lady came and told us it was by Hamish Miller and was all about standing stones, circles, energies, and dowsing. Geoff was intrigued. Needless to say the book was bought and in no time Geoff wanted some rods to try it for himself, starting with water. He dowsed for water everywhere. I recall that I once went to a homeopath for treatment. During our conversation she mentioned that they wanted to get a supply of water to the stables, but could not trace where the supply ran to or from. I volunteered Geoff's services. He was taken back a bit, as he had never taken on a project before. Nevertheless off he went with his rods and duly found that the pipe was below two other plastic pipes hence they were difficult to find. He gave them the order of the pipes, depth, and direction in which the water ran. The next thing we knew they had a big digger in the drive and were making a large hole in accordance with his directions. To everyone's delight all was exactly as Geoff had told them and in no time they had their water supply. That was all very exciting and happily proved Geoff to be a very precise dowser!

Here he is, working with his dowsing rod

It caused quite a stir at our bed and breakfast as guests saw what we did. Everyone was so interested and in time it became "bed, breakfast, healing and dowsing". We had great pleasure in showing our guests how to use rods and pendulums. I found that I worked better with a pendulum. Having said that I found a line through the altar in Glastonbury Cathedral with rods that Geoff and his friend had missed! There was a lot of fun and laughter, but also surprise when they found that with a little bit of help, they could use them too. Quite a few of them bought rods or pendulums for themselves, a whole new world opened up to them.

This is the third day of our holiday week away. Ken and I decided to go to Saint Michael's Mount. It really is a most fascinating place to visit. Spectacular views to look at, surrounded by the sea, masses of history, ghosts and ghostly stories. Apparently one ghost pulls the hair of visitors giving them quite a scare. Earthbound spirits, being another interest of ours, we were eager to hear more! It is one hell of a scramble getting up to the building itself but well worth the effort. I am afraid my poor old legs did complain quite a lot. I am so glad I got up there on my own steam though. It made everything feel perfect. The house is quaint and full of interesting things and from every window there are breathtaking views. How different they are from high up! It would have been nice to have a slide to go down on. Geoff and I have visited there several times and never been disappointed.

It just so happens that Saint Michael's Mount is on the route to a number of ancient stones, circles etc. Quite a few of which Geoff was doing research on for a book he was writing. This is what makes our visits to Cornwall so special (apart from coastal views of course) as it has featured so big a part in our dowsing, especially for Geoff. There are so many ancient sites of importance here. One in particular comes to mind: The Merry Maidens. This is a lovely circle, which we felt the need to visit often. Sadly to say on this occasion we were unable to go there, but the last time I went was with Geoff and was very special to me for a number of reasons, and was very exciting.

This time I was getting a little restless as Geoff was working on the stones longer than usual. A thought flashed through my mind, *Why don't I study them myself?* So I did. The first impression I got was that it was a very feminine circle, and after a while was aware of female adults and children, dancing in a procession into the ring. There were also very bright "spirit" people with them. I likened them to fairies. Everything was full of joy. I began to dowse the stones and was amazed to find each stone held a musical note. I jotted them down and showed them to Geoff. He promptly started to chuckle a little. I thought he was making fun of me but he assured me that was not so, and said, with an air of mystery, he would show me a passage in the book he was reading. Imagine my surprise to see a similar account in print by somebody else who had the same experiences. At least it took away the thought that it was just my imagination. I think Geoff was rather pleased to find how much my dowsing had improved.

The music of The Merry Maidens does not seem to be something you can easily call to mind. I tried several times without success. It just seems to come of its own volition. Strangely, about three weeks before my dear one passed on, the music came to me and kept going round and round in my mind and stopped as suddenly as it started when he departed from this earth. One other rather eerie thing is that it has come to me again two or three times since I have been here. I wonder what that portends? Something happier I hope.

Not much more of our holiday left. Where to next, I wonder?

It was to Porthleven, another super place. It has a very oldie worldie inn there, which looks as if it has been cut out of the cliffs. Its garden is laid out in tiers, which is rather nice as nowhere seems to get crowded. Funnily enough it is the first place Geoff noticed when we arrived here, and so did our son. It is a great garden. There are plenty of views and, therefore, very nice to try a little sketching. I did some myself but there is quite a bit of artistic licence in my picture.

Two friends have joined us for the last days of our stay. We visited some delightful little coves, full of motley boats bobbing up and down. Ken had a rest as his friends took on the driving. It was all so enjoyable but there was no space left for me to drift off with my thoughts – other than that I so wanted to stay a little longer here with my Geoff and our memories.

Saturday came all too soon and its back home again. We could not dawdle, as Geoff and I used to. Ken had a long journey to Somerset that day and then on to Kent early the next, but he tried to make the journey as pretty as possible. Returning home I will have to start re-thinking my life and what I have learned from this week away.

October comes and goes so quickly. There were beautiful

sunny days when it was a joy to go for a brisk walk to the sea. Often followed, very quickly, by heavy rain and grey depressing skies. I feel that I am being tested to the hilt for now I have the prospect of my daughter moving away from here. The only kin I have left nearby, and she has been such a pillar of strength for me during the past few difficult years. Sue and Nick only live about ten minutes' walk from here and now it is to be over thirty miles away. It is said that it is not so far away but once more things will never be the same again. There is something of a comfort feeling when your children live nearby, and the odd "pop in" for a cup of tea happens. Once they have to move away it usually ends up with seeing them less often, mainly because of the pressure of their work and so forth, but there is also the consideration that they have their own families to worry about and of course to visit. I hastily have to add that all my dear children do their very best to see me as often as possible and ring me regularly.

On the other side of the coin my pictures of the past are still coming, especially now as we head towards Christmas. All those cards that had to be written and sent! Preparing for Dunster by Candlelight, held in the first weekend of December. It was such a wonderful time for Geoff and I when we offered bed and breakfast. It was the big charity village event. We used to have four regular visitors plus two on a waiting list. It is a two-night event and we used to organise places to dine for them. In the morning, they would come down to a roaring log fire and carols for them to enjoy. On the Sunday morning, the day they were leaving, the ladies had a small box of chocolates and there was a little present for all of them to take home as a sort of souvenir. It became to be looked on as an early Christmas by our regular visitors and by our second year of being hosts they insisted that we should join them for the meal on Saturday – a tradition that continued for twelve years, the extra two guests always being keen to join us. They all had a good sense of humour, and my Geoff, with his lovely smile and easy manner, soon had them at their ease, happy and laughing into the small hours. They often brought us little Christmas gifts – so touching. It was hard work in some ways, but the joy far outweighed all else.

I had hoped to see my youngest son receive his doctorate in November but all plans had to be cancelled. Unbelievable, he and his wife are also moving – who said lightening never strikes twice. But I would love to have seen him get his doctorate. They are going from Worcester to a village outside of Leicester. I hope these children of mine will find happiness in their new abodes. Someone on high has seemingly decided that I am to make a completely new start to my life. So many changes but not much staying the same. There may be more family moves in the pipeline! I was feeling very isolated and alone in many ways when another happy event came to mind.

It is back in the middle of the 1990s. My mum and dad were with us for Christmas. Dad was very ill with cancer and both he and Mum were on a lot of pills. Bless them. They had become quite obsessed with their medication thinking of little else. I light heartedly said to my dad, 'Take the pills you have to take, then forget them for a while and we will have a happy time together,' which we did. Halfway through dinner a beautiful piece of John Rutter music came on the music centre. It was a compilation of music based on

Beatrice Potter characters, one of which was a lively, happy waltz. I am afraid I am a little impulsive sometimes – I put down what I was serving, pulled Geoff off his chair and waltzed him round and round the dining room table. My dear old dad and mum laughed so much they were in tears. They knew Geoff was not too comfortable with dancing, but on this occasion he enjoyed it very much. A little bit of happy madness. I am so happy it all went like that as I lost my dad about three weeks later.

As I have said before, our Cornish holidays were always special, but this one with Ken was extra special for it opened my mind to all the happy times Geoff and I had together. The wonderful things we learnt, and gifts received that we would use to help others. How blessed we had been, and I have now realised how very blessed I have been to have met and married my soulmate, which grew into such a loving and happy relationship for so many years. We were one.

Another Christmas, a few years back, Geoff came home from work and was so delighted with a song he had heard on the radio. It was 'When a Child was Born', I think that was its title, and was sang by Johnny Mathis. When I heard it I really understood why. It was all about the things we believed in, and hoped for, a world of peace, love, light and happiness, which could happen if we all showed respect to each other and less of the imposing of wills.

Since going away I find I am counting my blessings and trying to be more positive, which, thanks to my dear Cruse bereavement counsellor, is becoming easier. I will always feel the pain of the parting and I know I will continue to shed tears, but I am aware that he is always with me, guiding me and watching over me as I walk my path. There are still difficult times ahead, Christmas and the period when we were so rudely parted from each other. Equally, there are new challenges. In April, I am going to Austria with a dear young friend, Becky, who has also given me love and support. It is her first big trip abroad, so we will hold each other up as I take my first stumbling steps into the start of a very different life.

The Phoenix is slowly rising. It has a way to go but knows there is light at the end of the tunnel. I Wonder what the outcome of it all will be for me. Knowing that Geoff is with me and I am still loved and blessed, I can walk safely into the future. I feel he will guide me. The outcome, only time will tell, but it all looks promising. I hope I will have found myself, at least just a little.

And the journey goes on…

3. Getting to Know Me

I just cannot believe that it is already thirteen months since my darling husband passed away. How quickly time flies by, and yet, I feel as if it all happened only a week ago.

The lovely Cornish holiday I had with my Ken, was wonderful and set me on my feet for a while. Visiting all those familiar and very beautiful places we knew so well, and, of course, the wonderful memories built there, recalling such happiness and much laughter.

From September onwards it was a time of thinking of things to do with myself and about my family. I am afraid that birthdays and special occasions just went to the wall for a long time so I needed to sort that out. My beloved family did not deserve to be forgotten but that it how it goes when you are gradually losing your soulmate in such an unhappy manner. Then there was Christmas. Whatever will I do with myself! I could not imagine such a time without my Geoff sharing it with me. The idea of decorating the house, thinking of carols, festive meals and presents – for a long time, I just could not. Then the family stepped in. Bless them. The whole period was organised for me and I was to see all of them during the festive period. Suddenly I found myself looking for presents they would like and getting Christmas cards written for family and neglected friends, and so the time flew by, rather bittersweet, as I was still receiving lots of things addressed to both of us, but there were bright times to.

A little before Christmas I got a call from a lady who organises parcels for the needy and she invited me to give a hand with the Christmas load. I was a bit unsure at first but went along, taking a few items for them. It turned out to be a wonderful thing to be a part of, and fun in its way. A lovely group of people from our church raise money and food donations to help those less fortunate than themselves. The parcels were amazing, with not only the basic needs but Christmas cake, Christmas pudding, and even sweeties for the children. When filled, each box was beautifully decorated in a seasonal manner. I think they said they had reached a total of 300 parcels. Local people, churches and large stores all gave and still give so generously.

One things I thought was so wonderful was the masses of miniature knitted bootees and fabric boots lovingly made by a dear elderly lady. They were all filled with a few sweets for the parcels. Before going into the boxes we built them up into a sort of pyramid with festive decorations around and a card by the side. A photograph was taken and sent to the lady with lots of thanks for all her efforts. Bet the kiddies were delighted with them.

This was my first step towards finding myself – thinking of someone else's problems and forgetting mine for a little while.

I was to spend my first Christmas "alone" with Mark and Gina, who, at that time, lived in a super bungalow in beautiful Worcester, which had a very special and peaceful garden. It would be good to go there once more before their move to the village outside of Leicester.

On my arrival to their home, I was greeted by their dog Dylan. It was great to see that crazy old dog again. He fussed around me for quite a while as if he knew how I was feeling. He is a lurcher, mostly looking very lazy and sleepy, but when he was free to let go he was a beautiful sight of poetry in motion. He went at such a speed, and the sheer joy on his face as he leapt, bounded, ran and jumped was marvellous to behold. Quite uplifting.

The inside of their bungalow looked beautiful in its festive dress and the log burner was full of colourful dancing flames, emanating warmth and comfort – very welcoming. Gina had been very busy making all sorts of Christmas treats. They soon had me settled in, and reasonably relaxed. Over a glass of wine they told me that Gina's mum, dad and sister were coming Christmas Day. I looked forward to that. They are dear souls.

They took me to midnight Mass at a church not too far away. It was a bit of a disappointment really. Something was missing. In fact, a couple of some things were missing. I could put right the first one by thinking of those gathered at my local church. It has such a family-like feeling between the clergy and the congregation. It would be bright, warm, happy and full of love. The knowledge of which, in turn, made me happy. The second "something" was out of my hands, but I felt him near me all the time, as loving as ever. I would so love to have his hand holding mine then and always.

Back home we stayed up for a Christmas drink, a little television, a while later we went off to bed. This is the time when I still reach a low ebb and become a bit weepy.

Christmas Day duly came and the family arrived. It was great having them here. We all chatted together easily. In the evening, Mark got us all playing games and it really was fun. I was so glad they were staying over. We had a really lovely Christmas, but in spite of this, even with dear family around me, I was still getting that feeling of isolation – like being alone in a crowd – that drags me down and by the time I got to bed the pain of not having Geoff by my side was indescribable. I just cried and cried until I fell asleep.

Anyway, life has to go on. The next day parents and sister returned home and Gina and Mark's son, his wife and their very lively little girl came. She had a terrible cold, bless her, but it did not seem to stop her from having fun. She was quite a handful and very inquisitive. She had a real liking for mobile phones, etc. Perhaps she will grow up to be a telephone engineer one day! It was lovely watching her open all her parcels and it soon became obvious that she knew what she liked. It is great watching the antics of toddlers and how quickly they learn. However, bedtime came, and the little one was so congested she could not sleep. She cried quite a bit during the night. Strangely it was the first night in ages that I slept much better and was most surprised that no one else got any sleep at all. Oh boy, do I remember nights like that with my four young ones. I used to get fed up with Geoff, as he always managed to sleep all the way through it all.

There was a change of plan about how I was to return home. Sue and Nick were not going to be too far away and volunteered to drive me home, giving Mark a little rest from driving. They came and spent the night with us and it was super to see my family laughing and chatting together.

I don't know why but I suddenly felt in the way. After all, they were two couples who had not seen each other for a little while and probably had things they would like to talk about. I began to feel weepy – here it comes again –

that lost feeling because my sweetheart was not with me, will it ever ease? Mark spotted that something was up and asked what was troubling me. I told him what I was feeling and he would have none of it. He told me I was loved and wanted by all of them, indeed all of the family, and I was to sit down and join in the games with them. I am so glad that I did. We had such a good time. A game of Jenga, I think that is what it was called – it was hilarious. My lass had had a glass or two of Christmas cheer. She was so happy, bright as a button too. However, when we played the game above she completely forgot all about "gently" removing one piece without knocking the whole tower over. She kept poking it quite hard, and the look on her face when the whole lot tumbled down, was a picture. Such surprise and a little like a crestfallen little girl. She made me feel that I had my little five-year-old back for a while. I just wish I could find the words to draw the picture for all to see, but it set me laughing and laughing until I was in tears, which was commented on as I had not laughed like that for years. Strangely I think that it did everyone some good.

The next day came and it was all over. It had been such a nice, enjoyable break. Now we were all going our different ways, and the thought of returning home did not really feel all that good. After Sue and Nick had dropped me home things started to go downhill a bit. I missed the company and the encouragement terribly and naturally not having my Geoff being physically with me was predominant in my mind, making me feel very sad. On top of all this I knew I would be seeing and hearing a lot less from Sue and Nick when they moved away in about two weeks' time, and equally that it would be quite a time before I was to see Gina and Mark as their move was also imminent. I fretted because I had not heard from a couple of friends over Christmas and significant dates in the near future started to loom up: 1st January; 8th January, my birthday and the day upon which I had heard such awful news; 16th January, when Geoff went onto a pain-free and loving place; 24th January, the day of the funeral, and the day his ashes were given to me in a wicker pot. So much misery in such a short time! I began to become fearful about the holiday I was to go on in April, always feeling scared that I would get lost wherever I went – a thing I had not felt before. The children want me to go and visit them, but I was and am still having problems with going any distance on trains and buses. Therefore the children either collect me and take me to their homes or come to stay at mine, which is all a bit hard on them. Eventually I went to see my doctor. He put me on beta blockers but they made me feel so ill I had to come off them. I chose to try to go it alone for a while without medication, and see how I fared.

The children helped me through again. Sue visited me for a few hours on my birthday and took me out for lunch during which we had a nice chatty time, which helped tremendously. On 16th January, I went to Sue and Nick's home, where Nigel and Sue joined us. We were all together for the weekend. On the Saturday we went to Wells Cathedral. I had not been there for ages. Geoff and I went there a few years ago where, of course, he did some dowsing. It is not a massive building but very beautiful, and you get a lift when you visit there and come away feeling much more at peace with yourself. That previous time the cloisters were full of little charity stalls etc. and masses of people bustling around. So different this time.

In the evening, Sue and Nick took us all to the local, oldie village pub, which was full of friendly chatty people, just as the pubs were when we lived in Dunster. Sue did us proud. We had lovely meals, were well entertained, thus having a very happy weekend full of chat, and love, each knowing that Dad was very much in all our minds.

Sunday came, and once again, we all had to go our individual ways; Nigel and Sue to Bucks, and Nick took me home. Once again I was so very tearful, and was so glad when Chris phoned and asked if I would help out with the parcels on the Monday. Wonderful – helping others again kept me occupied.

I do get a lot of texts and phone calls from family and friends, which helps me a lot, but I am beginning to think I must try to do, or participate in other things if I am ever to come to terms with the finding of this "new way of life" that has been thrust upon me!

Late in January, my friend Gail's father introduced me to the bereavement club he goes to – I call it the Friendship Club – as that is exactly what it is. I was helped quite a bit by a lady under an umbrella who thought I looked "friendly and chatty" and started to converse with me. It was quite funny really because we found we were both going to the same place. She was one of the group. It took me a little while to settle in but they were all such pleasant people it did not take too long.

Now I have started on two new ventures which feels good, yet I was getting more depressed at home and it was getting worse.

I think that the weather plays a part in it. So much rain. Grey skies. Waking up and going to bed in the dark.

I think many people get depressed at this time of the year. Everything is so gloomy and there seems to be so little good news. So we could do without all this when we are losing our special ones. It makes it all so much harder to bear.

In the meantime my children were trying to persuade me to go to the doctor again and ask for a little help before things get too bad. Eventually I succumbed and made an appointment.

When I went to see him he was very kind and understanding. It was pointed out that I had carried quite a load for quite a long time. It was something like four years – I think. He said I was on the brink of being clinically depressed, which is what I was afraid of. He suggested a mild antidepressant for a short time and to see how I get on, which I accepted although I do not really like taking pills much. Fortunately a couple of my children had been on them and warned me that I would feel worse before getting better. Glad they told me as I felt awful for some little while; nausea and tummy troubles for most of it. In fairness it was as they said. I was very sleepy most of the time. Sleeping at night and quite a bit during the day – such a rest I had not had in ages. All this extra rest gave me extra strength, especially in my legs, so I decided I would take them for a bit longer and see how it worked out.

What bliss. We are having some lovely sunny, summer-like days. Quite warm too. At last, able to go for a good walk and feel the warmth of the sun on me. Needless to say my first thought was to get down to the sea. I was surprised to see so many people, especially children playing on the beach or walking along the proms, and in the shops too. It looks as if we have all been called out by the sun. What a bonus in February. I took a walk to the harbour; the tide was in, so I had a snack at the cafe whilst enjoying watching the boats bobbing about on the startling blue sea, the mount on which Dunster seems to stand, and the gorgeous hills all around. I sat there for quite a time, and would you believe it, I actually got a little sunburnt! Almost without noticing one or two grey clouds had started to appear and a little wind was building up. I tossed up whether to go to Culver Cliff or return home. Culver Cliff won. I sat there in the quiet for a long time. Quite a bit too long I was to find as just within two turnings from home the skies opened and I got drenched. Never mind, it was well worth it. I had enjoyed every minute of it.

7th March came, Geoff's and also my brother's birthday but also the day Geoff's ashes were interred. My Ken came to stay with me and help me to get through this period. I am so glad he did, and also that the pills were showing signs of helping me as I was not quite so dozy now and was crying less.

Ken came on the day before and promptly took me for a drive over the hills. I love the moor. There is so much to see: deep valleys with farms tucked away in them, gorgeous views of changing landscapes; and of course the sea and boats. If you are lucky enough you may come across a group of Exmoor ponies, such beautiful creatures, along with free roaming sheep and cattle, which have huge curved horns. I think they may come from Scotland, I am not sure, but although they look fierce I gather they are gentle. I will take their word for it.

We went back via Dunster where we had a sociable pint for Ken and red wine for me, before going home for a bit of tea and a relaxing evening watching TV.

On 7th, Ken took me to Geoff's little grave. I took some pink roses and put them around the silk ones. It was so peaceful and his grave looked so pretty. I wonder what people think of his little windmill in the midst of the flowers gently blowing in the wind.

After this he took me to Lyme Regis where we had a tasty snack and a drink at the inn on the seafront. The weather was great which delighted us and gave us great joy, for this was a favourite place of Geoff's and mine, and Ken, along with his brothers and sister, grew up coming both here and Charmouth to stay with their Nan and Grandad, holidaying three or four times a year. What a lucky family to grow up with such heavenly holidays, which I certainly did not have when I was a little child. Before returning home we went to Charmouth, which was just a short distance along the coast. We shared such happy memories, such as the smashing tearooms just off the beach with its pretty lawns and flowers (now under a block of apartments called Tea Gardens) everything there was homemade and the cakes melted in your mouth. Then there was Barney's Cafe and Fossil Shop – a fascinating place for my young ones, very interesting.

Our last full day together was spent locally, mainly along the seafront. We had a meal at the Ship Aground, which was very enjoyable. The time just flew by and by 11am the next day he was on his way home. He was a dear to take me out so much. The day he took me over the moors he had just driven up from Kent.

A few days later it is Mothers' Day and I went to church. The service was very special. They played the Crucifixion with people in the congregation reading the parts. It was so very touching. To top it all, the children came round with baskets of pots of primroses, one for each mother and grandmother present. It was so moving as it was obviously very important to the children to be chosen to present them. They looked quite proud of themselves. Yet another surprise came with the coffee as we had a slice of simnel cake waiting for us when we all met in the narthex after the service. I came away both lifted and happy but still wishing for one more little miracle.

None of my family were able to be with me but on the Thursday prior to Mothers' Day my dear lass rang and said Nick would be collecting me and taking me to their place for an overnight stay as they could not be with me on the day. I had a great meal and a glass of wine that evening followed by a bit of TV viewing and a chat. When I went up to bed there waiting for me was a huge bouquet of sweet-smelling flowers and a really special card. Again I felt very touched. How lovely of them to think of me.

Saturday morning, on my arrival home, I was met with another colourful arrangement of flowers. This time arranged on an oasis and they came from Mark and Gina, again with a lovely card.

Nigel and Sue sent me a DVD of *Maleficent* and Ken a DVD of *Philomena*, both wonderful to watch, and again accompanied with loving cards. What a lucky mum I am to be thought of like this by them all. I still wish one of them could have been with me though. Geoff used to take me out for dinner on Mothers' Day, often followed by a drive over the moors, where we stopped for an ice cream and a look out to sea halfway. Funnily he totally disapproved of Fathers' Day – I think on religious grounds. I have got that missing feeling again. It is always there but sometimes, on special occasions it gets too much to bear!

Every now and then something special happens when you can help someone in distress but at the end of the day it has also helped you. It was one of those grey but warm sort of days and I thought it would be nice to walk to Culver Cliff viewing point and think about my dear old Geoff. Coming up to the small, rather awkward roundabout just before this nature reserve I came upon a chap whose buggy had completely broken down and he was stranded for he had no movement below his waist, which I think he said was due to polio. He told me his partner had gone to get the relevant transport to get him home. I felt it was a rather dangerous situation to be in so suggested that I stay and chat to him until she came back. We got to know each other quite well and found that they only lived around the corner from me. Small world! In a while his lady came along, released the brakes and I helped her to push the buggy over to their vehicle. The buggy was quite heavy so I am pleased that I waited for her. After all this I went and sat at the viewpoint and felt my man close by me and equally felt such warmth and happiness for being able to give a hand out. After a little while the weather had changed. By now the sky had turned quite grey, the wind very strong and big rolling waves crashing on the shore. It is a great joy watching a big sea but it was also getting terribly cold and the light was going. Best to get on the road and back home I think.

When I returned home I had a lovely surprise for attached to the handle of my front door was a pretty bunch of flowers and a card thanking me for caring. What a lovely thought. There are some really special l people out there.

On the spiritual path, things are happening. Geoff and I have always had a deep belief in the afterlife, healing, complementary medicine and so forth. Since my love's passing so many things have happened. My healing energy is so much stronger, as expressed by those who have been in receipt of it, and I must admit that I am aware of some sort of development in myself. Also I very much feel Geoff's presence and somehow I know he is working with me, which is truly wonderful.

On one occasion my daughter put Radio 2 on as she felt that pop music would cheer me up. I am afraid the music they were playing at the time did quite the opposite. I thought I would do some work in the kitchen so that all I got was a quieter version of it. All of a sudden, about fifteen minutes later, I heard some really lovely music being played and was so surprised that this channel played such music. It was so peaceful and relaxing I sat down to listen to it. Imagine my amazement when a voice said, 'This is Classic FM.' I was the only one in the house! Geoff never did like pop music! A similar thing happened when Becky and I sat and watched a DVD. Without any warning it reverted back to TV. That happened twice and never again since! There is so much we do not understand about life – thought provoking, eh?

Friday 20th March: I have had the good fortune to see the first eclipse for sixteen years. It was both amazing and eerie. The light became very subdued and it got quieter and quieter as it reached the full eclipse. What an event to watch from my bedroom window. It will not be seen again for ninety years, I gather, so I am most unlikely to be there! You really can understand why it was held in such awe in the distant past. Geoff and I were on a high hill late at night when the previous eclipse took place sixteen years ago. It really went black and you could hardly see the others up there with us. One minute there were a few birds twittering, geese honking and dogs barking. The next minute it all fell silent apart from one buzzing little fly that they had obviously forgotten to "put into the picture."

A couple of days later, Becky came for an overnight stay. She does that sometimes to give me a bit of companionship, and she tells me that she really rather enjoys these trips. We chatter together over a meal, and then we enjoy a good DVD, finishing off with a phone chat with Roy, my brother-in-law – all good relaxing stuff.

The following morning it was so sunny and warm we decided to go for a good long walk after breakfast. It was heavenly walking by the sea with the warmth of the sun on our backs. Out of the blue we happened on another historical event here in Minehead. It was the furthest the sea had gone out for 260 years. Incredible. How it was that we had no knowledge of this heaven only knows, but I am so glad that we did not miss it. From where we were standing, the gap between here and Wales looked like a river. The stumps of ancient trees could be seen so the forest obviously extended very far out to sea. There was also evidence of how people fished for their livelihoods all those years ago. Quite humbling to think that people like Becky and I were standing where people lived and worked as we do but on ground we now view as the sea, proms and beaches. Again it is something that will never be seen again for many, many years. I wonder how much more land will be engulfed by the sea many years hence. I wish my Geoff had been here to share these remarkable events with me. No doubt out he would come with his rods and he would be lost in thought for quite a while. How lovely that would have been.

A gentleman who understood about these events took parties right to the edge of the sea, showed them all the important things to note and explain them. Quite a lot of people took up these trips. Glad no one got caught on the incoming tide, which comes in at quite a rate.

We watched things for quite a while then decided we were getting a bit hot and tired so went off to find a tearoom. We found a very special one with fantastic wall colours and comfy armchairs as well as tables and chairs. The tea was beautifully served, along with a tasty piece of homemade cake and we happily relaxed listening to jazz music on their player. My dear one and I were very keen on modern jazz. It was all gorgeous – the icing on the cake at the end of a splendid day.

This is the day I have both feared and wondered about: the start of the Austrian trip. What will it be like? No Geoff – Becky and I going together, both searching for something. It is a long, long way away!

The few days before were chaotic with so much to do in readiness. Keys to get cut for my neighbours, handbag to be re-sewn, trousers to be repaired and tit bits for the coach journey. Finally setting watches for teaming up and setting off, Becky's father kindly agreeing to drive us up to the collection point. By the end of all this, I realised I was beginning to look forward to the trip, and to finding what I was made of. At the same time I also became incredibly emotional, constantly breaking into tears. How mixed up is that? I must get to bed early, very early, and get myself calmed down, and more relaxed. Help! I made calls to all my children, or they to me, rang Roy and then to bed at 9.20pm. Unbelievable. Becky was to give a wake-up call at 3.30am but when it came I was already awake. However, I did get a few hours sleep and woke up feeling a little better.

At 4.40am we were on our way, complete with butterflies in our tummies. A small coach collected us and by 5.05am we were off to collect one other couple before going on to Taunton to join the main coach. It was super, and had all the facilities, which also provided a tasty hot chocolate, tea, coffee, or soup at regular intervals. We were soon to find that the staff and fellow passengers were lovely and easy to get on with. Suddenly everything felt right, both for Becky and myself. I was feeling calm and, although just a little apprehensive, was enjoying the prospect of things to come. I knew my Geoff would be happy to see me stepping out, making the effort to do things that would fulfil me a little and also make me a little happier.

When we reached Dover we found we were to be on one of the two new ferries. It was massive. It was quite an experience. The interior was very swish and again vast. The experience was a little bewildering at first but we were soon taken up with looking at the White Cliffs of Dover, at the same time feeling the ferry coming to life beneath us and pulling away from port. There were lots of ships and boats to look at to. Out came the cameras and picture-taking began; the start of building new memories to mingle with the old. Now our journey has really begun.

We arrived at Calais at about midday. Everything went smoothly at customs and almost before realising it we were on the road to Liege in Belgium. Here we were to stay for our first night. It was a long ride and we did not realise how much of Belgium we were going to see. The Blakes' drivers were a mine of information and kept us well informed all through the journey, which everyone appreciated. They had a terrific sense of humour to. The weather was a little sad, mist and light rain, but we enjoyed the journey. Furthermore my brain was kicking in a bit and I was quite easily adjusting to euro money and paying the toilet entry in cents? Just as well as there were quite a few comfort stops on the way! Our hotel was a Weston; very comfortable and good food. I slept quite well, to my surprise.

The following day we drove on to, and across, Germany. The ice train airport at Frankfurt was pointed out to us. It was colossal and very cleverly designed. We learnt the high command of the Luftwaffe was in this region and later where the military high command had been during the war.

Going past Cologne we just saw the three spires of the cathedral as it was shrouded in mist, and were told it had the largest bell in Europe. Wish I had been able to see more of it. Also we were shown the area in which Schindler lived. What a brave man he was.

The first sighting of the Danube River truly took my breath away. I had always dreamed of seeing this river as my grandmother used to waltz me around the lounge to the strains of 'The Blue Danube Waltz'. It really was blue! Oh, those happy days when I was very small. How my Geoff would have appreciated this spot!

Funny, as I talk of him the memories of happiness are coming back, of warm and loving times shared together and less of the tearful thoughts. We both adored Austria and I really think it is helping me to appreciate the happiness we shared here instead of the sorrows of parting. Even though we are still en route I can feel it pulling at my heart strings. All is going to be well.

One of the great joys for Becky and I was the changing of the scenery and architecture we were seeing on these two days on the road. At first very flat but such verdant land along with trees and shrubs all along the way looking so pretty. Everything so orderly and clean. The changing church spires enthralled us, many with sharp, pointed spires, and others globe-like, going into a sort of small point, almost eastern in their appearance. Everywhere looking so beautiful.

The houses became to look more like musical boxes with their balconies, beautiful murals and flowers all around as we got closer to the Austrian border. I must admit some of the viewing was lost to quite a few forty winks as we felt so tired, but we tried hard not to miss anything along this stretch as it was far too beautiful to miss; we may have felt tired but we also felt oh so good. We were doing it – making new and stronger starts in life. Becky is already absolutely blooming, this area working its usual magic for we are now in Austria.

We arrived in glorious sunshine at our pretty hotel in St. Georgen im Attergau. We felt happy just looking at it. Our evening meal was set for 7.30pm. So we really only had time for a quick wash and brush up. When we went into our room we were over the moon; it was so light, spacious and with pretty views from the windows. Our home for the next five nights. We felt so lucky!

The dining room was very homely with the sound of lots of happy voices chattering away. We had, the previous day, made friends and sat with Jo, which was a real pleasure. Tonight we were to join Peter and Ann at their table, we had all met up on the smaller coach when we started out. We had a tremendous evening and a very happy one, a glass of red wine soon dispensing with any shyness. After a further glass of wine, followed by an unexpected welcome drink from the hotel, it was about 11.30pm. A need was felt to go to bed, and we were pleased to snuggle down. Had another good sleep but the room was rather warm so I woke up a little early feeling very clammy – a small price to pay.

The hotel has a most super dog. He is huge, and when we came upon him on the landing in the half-light he looked a bit frightening. Getting to know him we found him to be the most loving, gentle old thing but I would not like to be an intruder. He came with us on the guided tour of the village, kindly given by the owner of the hotel, and I think he came up to each one in turn as we wandered around. The village proved to be quite charming and still has buildings going back before 1400-odd. We also saw how they housed their cattle here, who were amazingly tame and friendly towards us.

Sadly, the weather had been pretty bad, but we did not let ourselves get down. After visiting the beautiful and lovingly built village church we wandered around getting to know the area better. We found a cafe, which looked most welcoming, so we went in out of the rain and got warmed up by a tasty hot chocolate. We got talking to a couple of local men who very kindly took a picture of us when we asked. I even tried out a little Austrian on them. They were so pleased with my efforts, they even understood me, and I came away with a little more confidence than I had before.

I reckon my Geoff will be really pleased with my progress and that I had spoken to them in their own language. After our drink and chat with the locals we had a further walk but the weather was really getting a bit much and we were very wet so we found our way back to the hotel, which was an achievement in itself, and enjoyed a relaxing writing session whilst appreciating yet another hot chocolate. Yummy! Won't be long before the evening meal.

Our meal was really good and full of surprises. We had bread soup for starter – a first for me – and I am not sure what the main meal comprised of, but it was vegetarian, made of all local produce, and was jolly tasty. Another pleasant surprise was to follow. We were given a slide show and narrative of the im Attergau Salzkammergut region. The whole thing was breathtaking with its views of mountains, some still shrouded in snow, huge forest areas, gorgeous sparkling rivers and pastures covered with a colourful variety of wild flowers, such as our land used to have when I was little. I never guessed what a variety of animals lived here in the forests: red squirrels, deer, wolves, and wild cats the size of which I never dreamt of, along with birds of prey and so on. It seemed endless. It makes you wonder what might be watching you from behind the curtains of the forest when you were out for a walk. Had a chat with Peter and Ann at the end of the show, which we all enjoyed very much. Later we were quite pleased to be getting into bed after having such a full and wonderful day.

Today is the day I have so been looking forward to. It is the day of the train trip up the mountain. I have not felt so excited for ages – just like a little girl. When we saw the dear little train that was to take us up, we could only feel wonder and awe that such a small engine could push two carriages full of people up a steep mountain. What skill must have gone into the designing of it.

I was not to be disappointed; the marvel of it all, the constant changing of the scenery, literally from moment to moment, right up to the summit. The boarding area was surrounded by green fields, pastures, mountains and lakes, which were bright blue and sparkling, made you feel good as you were taking it all in. Gradually as we got further up there were thick forests, which opened to give an occasional peep of the mountains and lakes. The higher we went the more the mountains became enshrouded by mist. It was as if some of them had a misty ring just below the peak. Finally we saw more and more snow and fewer trees. What a wonderful sight it was.

By the time we got to the top there was a lot of snow on the ground and the mountains we were looking down at also had a thick covering of snow. They were so majestic.

It was quite a haul to the restaurant on the top with a winding path and slippery snow, to get to them. Needless to say I found a very skiddy patch and found myself on my back end. Normally I would have got up as soon as possible, assured everyone I was fine and did not need any help, rushing on feeling very foolish but on this occasion I saw the funny side of things. I laughed so much it was a job to get up at all. What a picture I must have made sliding around on the wet snow, but two strong hands soon had me upright again.

Our trip up the mountain on a train, two pals exploring together: Becky and I.

Jean Tymms

Jean Tymms

We walked, or slid, around the top, breathing in the clean fresh air and admiring the fantastic views of such a variety from snow-capped mountains, down to the fields and lakes far below. It was stupendous. It took my breath away. I was totally staggered when I saw how the building was built into the mountain. It was a sheer drop: a sight not to forget. Inside, the coffee and apple strudel was pretty good too. This is one day neither Becky nor I will ever forget. It was absolute bliss.

We crowded in so many things in the five days in Austria. We had a trip to Salzburg, which is quite a lot smaller than its capital, Vienna, but seems to have so much more history – at least that's how I saw it. On arriving we were divided into two groups, each being put in to the care of a guide who took us around for a couple of hours. There was so much to see: the fortress on the hill, where Mozart was born; and another apartment where he lived; the Street of Signs; not forgetting the beautiful church and square. We were shown a bridge that had padlocks of various shapes, colours and sizes all over it. We understood they were put there by sweethearts and lovers. At the end of the guided tour we had some time to ourselves. We found a great little shop where you can buy authentic Mozart chocolate balls. Just had to buy some of those. This is where we had to start finding our navigational skills to get to where we had to meet the coach. We made it, and not by the route the guide gave us, by so doing we found the graveyard and grave of one of Mozart's relatives. What a pair of clever clogs. Now home to a special five-course traditional Austrian meal. Hope the walking around will give us enough room to manage it.

What a treat. We went to Mondsee and its breathtaking

lake. We visited St Michael's church where Maria and Captain Von Trapp were married – as seen in the Sound of Music of course. I lit a candle for my Geoff there. We had been there together once and I felt him with me so strongly. Even Becky felt he was with us. I had to sit quietly for a while. It felt so good.

We were in luck for today was May Day in Mondsee and the local band, all wearing traditional costume, marched through the town. It sounded and looked grand. They went through the town once then returned through the town stopping outside each building, played a piece of music after which they were greeted by the proprietors. I hazard a guess they were given some sort of support for the band, but I am not completely sure of that. Had a hot chocolate – again – sat back and enjoyed it all very much. The music was happy and brought out the child in us all. Wanting to skip along behind the band as they marched.

The first time Geoff and I came to Austria we stayed in Sole in the Tyrol, the very thought of which brings me such happy memories. I remember it felt like visiting fairyland. Three of my children had never, like myself, been abroad at all, our eldest just pipping us to the post by going there for a short while earlier in the year. Geoff had been there with his parents when he was quite young. Whatever, we were all going and all enjoyed our "first" together. Right at the beginning of the holiday, the cattle were being brought down from the high pastures and were garlanded with flowers around their horns and carried a bell around their necks. The bells made a super sound as they came through the village followed by villagers in traditional clothes. The priests and other members of the church followed them and stopped at each station of the cross. I guess it was a religious ceremony but at the moment I cannot quite remember anything accept our excitement and joy – and that it was such a warm, sunny day. The atmosphere was so special and will live with me forever. Such precious golden memories. My daughter was just fourteen at the time, and whilst there met, and much later married, a chap from Cornwall. It must have all been written in the stars. Needless to say, none of us were in a hurry to come home. We just did not want to break that magical thread we had found. Now here I am again, oh so happy to be here. I now have new memories to add to the old.

Our first visit to 'Fairyland'

How quickly time flies when you are happy. All ready the time has come to pack our things in readiness for our departure tomorrow, and the first stage of our journey home. Once again I do not really want to go home, not yet. Neither does my little friend. We have been such a good team together. I love it here, and all my memories are, in the main, so happy. On the other hand, I do not feel I could keep up this pace for many more days. I am not as young as I used to be. Not in the flesh anyway.

We had another tasty breakfast in the morning – I will really miss that when I get home – after which we said our farewells to the hotel staff. Then off again to Liege, this time on a slightly different route so we were still receiving interesting bits of information. We arrived at the hotel at about 8pm, it doesn't seem five minutes ago that I was getting excited about my forthcoming experience in Austria; the finding of a new path to follow, or at least one that will be a little easier than that of the past months. I feel I have found some purpose for still being here, which restores a little self-worth. I was told my still being here was to do with me and the things I still have to do. I believe I am beginning to see a little light through the trees but I need more time to think about it all.

In a way our evening meal was a sad time. Becky and I sat with a different group this night. We all got on so well, happily laughing and chattering with each other. It did not feel right; tomorrow evening we would all be saying our goodbyes and going different ways. I think a lot of us felt that way. We were with a great group of people who got on so well. Wonder if any of us will meet up again. Would be nice, but it does not often happen. Without being aware of it they played a part in aiding my healing and steps forward. I am so grateful to them all. Bedtime, I am getting emotional again? Time for the land of dreams before the final journey to Calais, the ferry and home.

We enjoyed the return ferry trip very much. It was a good crossing and for a lot of the time we were in good company – a lovely couple, full of laughter. We were sorry to say goodbye to them. We spent the rest of the time looking at the shops on board, like having a floating Taunton! But the shops reminded me of the stop we had on our way through Belgium. We stopped at the Belgium Chocolate Factory; a child's delight and quite a temptation to adults as well to spend too much. Chocolates, in all shapes and colours. Made it a very difficult job trying to choose a few! Just as well we are limited on what we can carry!

Returning home was unbearable. Becky had her family eager to see her and hear all about her holidays. My home did not feel like a home. It felt very cold and empty and there was no one to talk to about my time away, what I had found, even about some of the daft things I did. Found myself crying a lot once again. I spoke to my four children later in the evening and they were so proud of me, I felt brighter for a while. I had done it; I had been there, found myself a bit, enjoyed it and even got the t-shirt! However, I was still a bit mixed up for a few days. It did not help that I felt really unwell shortly after I came back. I had picked up the flu-like virus that seems to be going around. After using a remedy of my grandmother's, hot tea, honey, and a couple of spoonfuls of whisky (the trouble is I was getting to enjoy the taste) I began to pick up a bit. In truth, the remedy really worked. Rather good that it also became enjoyable to take.

Naturally I had to rest up for a while but that was good for me. I had time to think more deeply into what I had achieved by setting this challenge for myself and carrying it through.

Going back through the period, I recall that after those two or three special days we had in Austria by the time I got to bed I was almost ashamed of enjoying myself so much. Why should I be having such a happy time? There were a few silent tears as I drifted off to sleep. Little thoughts were still in the back of my mind. Geoff should still be here with me!

Then out of the blue I re-felt the way I felt every day in Austria but about the times Geoff and I had been there, the companionship, the joy of it all. The house felt suddenly warmer too. I cannot explain it, it just did. I was becoming more and more aware of Geoff around me, and sometimes saw or heard him, occasionally both together, still guiding me and helping me. Bless you, my dear heart.

So this brings me to the end of my little ramblings. The holiday, the peak of these sad months made me, and has given me a starting point on which to build. I know my family are planning a number of visits in the next few months. More tests. Getting anywhere over here is more frightening than going to Austria – ah! *But*, this is a different story, which will be written as life goes on, but this time it will be for me! Wish me well.

Jean Tymms

Jean Tymms

Afterword

The following poem, written by my daughter, Sue Hutt, eloquently sums up how the whole family felt about Geoff in their individual ways. Be it brother, sons, friends – anyone who met him – all were drawn to his ready smile, old-world charm and great kindness. The world is a sadder place since he passed away.

Glimpses of Days Gone By

Your lovely voice reading me *Wind in the Willows*
Long walks in the Welsh countryside
'Just around the corner,' you would say
These things I remember and thank you for.

A kind and generous spirit looking after me
Eves that shone with love and pride
A face that shared my joys and pain
These things I remember and thank you for.

Always knowing you were there for me
Sat at the bar talking and making my world a happier place
Laughter echoes in my mind like sunshine on a rainy day
These things I remember and thank you for.

Talking through each day's newspaper
Doing the crossword and taking such joy in completion
Laughing at Butlin's and the antics of Mr Hare
These things I remember and thank you for

Visiting coffee shops to break up your day
Watching every antique show on TV
Sharing your memories and ideas for further adventures
These things I remember and thank you for.

To be a part of loving and caring for you
Was a privilege and blessing
To witness your courage and determination until the end
These things I remember and thank you for.

I always felt loved by you, Mr Waggins
I treasured our friendship
I am blessed to have had such a wonderful close relationship
    with my daddy
This I will always remember and thank you for.

Afterword continued

On a card I found a lovely verse that just seemed to sum up the way Geoff and I felt about each other. How, over the years, we grew as soulmates as well as friends, and so on.

Sadly it proved difficult to obtain permission to have it included in my book due to copyright. However, it told of how at the start we think it is all romance and passion, but as time goes on we realise it is the mundane things from which love really grows so strong, such as sitting in the dark by a log fire holding hands and watching the flames dancing in the hearth; the little secret jokes we share; reading books in bed together; and hugging up to each other when we are cold, such ordinary things but oh so important. It all comes down to sharing our lives together so that love develops and matures like a rare brandy. How lucky we were to share just such a life.

Acknowledgements

A great big thank you to all my family who have, and still are, helping me get through this painful period. I have leant on them quite heavily. Love and blessings to you all.

Thanks go to dear Roy, my brother-in-law, who is largely responsible for getting me to publish my "thoughts", giving me encouragement, guidance and part-funding of the project. Hotly pursued by Becky Cook, my dear friend, who kept the pressure on and gave me a great deal of assistance. Giuliana Fenwick for her advice and support. Janet Powels for keeping me "on track". And Kelly Creech for her friendship, help and terrific fundraising on my behalf for Myeloma UK. I've got some very persuasive and determined friends.

JEAN